M000288404

SEA KAYAK
HANDLING

Doug Cooper

A PRACTICAL MANUAL

First published 2009

Published in Great Britain 2009 by Pesda Press
Unit 22, Galeri
Doc Victoria
Caernarfon
Gwynedd
LL55 1SQ

ISBN: 978–1–906095–18–5

Printed and bound in Poland. www.polskabook.pl

THE AUTHOR
Doug Cooper

Doug has managed to spend a lifetime playing and working in the outdoors! Whether on the sea, surf, rivers or mountains he is at his happiest when exploring new parts of the world or challenging himself and others to improve their skills; this he has been doing for over twenty years. With a constant lust for adventure, Doug has sea kayaked all over the world including Greenland, Iceland, Norway's Lofoten Islands, Canada, Ireland, Scotland, Wales, Corsica, Sardinia and Croatia. His whitewater kayaking and mountaineering has also taken him on adventures around the globe.

At present Doug works as Head of Paddlesport at Glenmore Lodge, Scotland's National Outdoor Centre. Here his love of helping others learn and improve is met every day, when he works as a BCU Level 5 Sea and Whitewater Coach, Level 4 Surf Coach and a Mountain and Ski Instructor. In addition to this, Doug co-authored Scottish Sea Kayaking (Pesda Press), a selective guide to sea kayaking in Scotland.

Wherever it is in the world, if it involves exploring, learning and coaching you will find Doug with a smile on his face, enjoying his outdoor life!

ACKNOWLEDGEMENTS

Producing a book like this would be impossible if it were not for a lot of people who helped me during my years of paddling. My first thanks would have to go to my parents who have supported me in my love of adventure throughout my life, and have always been happy to find out what happened after the adventure! I would also like to thank Dawn for her patience and support whilst I was writing the book, without this it would not have been possible.

This thanks to Dawn must also be extended to her photographic expertise and capturing of the majority of the photos in the book, which would not have been the same without her constant support in endless photo shoots. Thanks to Ian Sherrington for the intro photograph to Chapter 9. Thanks also to Dave Rossetter and Claire Scott for their input on the Foundation Skills chapter. To name the coaches and sea kayakers who have helped, inspired, coached and questioned me over the years when off and on the water would be a book in itself, however they know who they are and I thank you all. Without you my knowledge of sea kayaking would not be where it is today.

Finally, thanks to Franco and Peter at Pesda Press, who have offered technical support and knowledge throughout and have produced a professional product.

INTRODUCTION

The sea kayak has evolved over many generations from the Inuit forbearers to the modern-day manufacturers. It does not matter if you are manoeuvring your sea kayak in a tight space at the back of a cave, undertaking a long open crossing, surfing onto a sandy beach, battling with strong winds or enjoying millpond conditions; the sea kayak has evolved to cope with it all. All too often, however, instead of our sea kayak feeling like a perfectly evolved craft that dances on the oceans, it feels like a troublesome barge with a mind of its own. If you can relate to this, then unfortunately the old adage "a poor worker always blames their tools" is most probably not far from the truth!

In this book we will look at the key skills that will enable you to handle your sea kayak in a variety of ways in a variety of conditions. We will examine the four core concepts for efficient sea kayak handling: posture, connectivity, power transfer and feel. These will help you to adapt each of the strokes and skills to meet your own individual needs and equipment. Every sea kayaker will end up developing a range of slightly different and individualised kayak handling skills. There is never a single 'right' way, just a more efficient way for each and every sea kayaker.

For video clips of each of the techniques discussed in the book, visit: pesdapress.com/seakayakhandling

By understanding and practising the following skills, you and your sea kayak will soon be dancing in harmony on the world's oceans.

CONTENTS

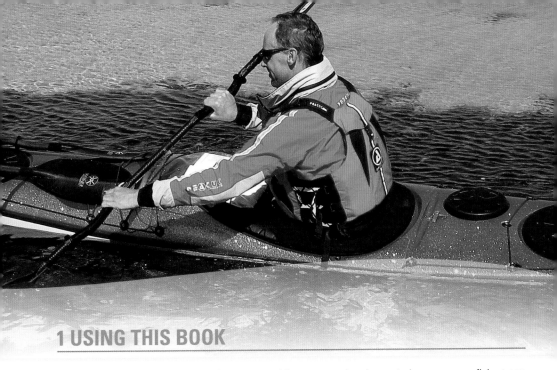

1 USING THIS BOOK

This book is not designed to teach you everything you need to know to become a proficient sea kayaker. The beauty of sea kayaking is that it draws together a variety of skills that allow the paddler to explore the fantastic coastlines around us. These skills include knowledge about equipment, safety, rescue, navigation, tidal planning, seamanship and weather. This book assumes that you have this knowledge (or are happy to paddle with someone who does) and are simply looking to develop your sea kayak handling skills to efficiently paddle the journeys you choose to undertake.

This book also makes the assumption that you have already learnt the necessary basic skills of launching, landing and staying upright in a sea kayak. In addition, it assumes that you are confident and comfortable in your kayak and know what to do in the event of capsize. One clear omission from this book is the skill of rolling a kayak; this would require a book in itself and there are already such publications out there.

With all this considered I hope that you will enjoy developing your sea kayaking skills through reading, understanding and practising what is in the book.

Equipment and environmental considerations

As any sea kayaker will know, every kayak is different and the weather and sea create an ever-changing environment. Skills will need to be adapted to suit these different sea kayaks and environmental conditions. To help with this there are additional information boxes that outline considerations in relation to the equipment used and the conditions paddled in. This will help you to modify the skills accordingly.

Learning and developing your skills

Some of you will be new to sea kayaking and learning these skills for the first time, and some of you may have been sea kayaking for years and looking at refining your skills. Either way, to develop new skills you will need to allocate plenty of time for practice. This will enable you to perform these skills in all situations without thinking. There are a few 'top tips' I can offer to ensure that this journey to skilful paddling is as smooth as possible.

By following these simple rules you will get the most from the book and your practice sessions.

- Do not focus on too many skills at one time.

- Practise on your left and right sides all the time.

- Start learning skills in an environment you feel comfortable in.

- Once you become competent at performing skills in a comfortable environment, change the environment to something more challenging.

- Practise your skills little and often, so that you do not overtire.

- When practising, try varying the speed, range and power used.

- Have someone observe and give feedback on what your skills look like in comparison to the pictures in the book.

- Have someone take photos or a video of you performing your skills; you can then compare these to the book.

This book will improve your understanding of the skills covered and enable you to 'self coach'. However, you will progress even quicker if you also have some quality coaching from a qualified coach – a worthwhile investment.

Buoyancy aids

In many of the photographs in the book the kayaker is not wearing a buoyancy aid. This is for the purpose of clearly showing the kayaker's body position and rotation and in no way is a recommendation for not wearing a buoyancy aid. The author would recommend that a buoyancy aid is worn at all times when sea kayaking.

ONLINE VIDEO CLIPS

You can view video clips of each of the techniques detailed in the book online at:

www.pesdapress.com/seakayakhandling

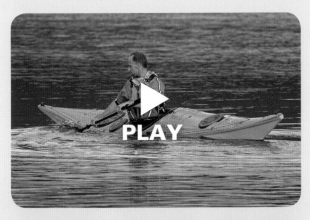

2 FOUNDATION SKILLS

There are four key concepts that paddlers should be aware of at all times while paddling.

Posture

Good posture.

Good posture is essential to avoid injury and maximise efficient performance. Achieving good posture should start at your pelvis and lower back. Ensure that your lower back is not rounded, but that your pelvis is tilted slightly forward and the core strength of your stomach is engaged in maintaining this. This should allow your upper body to maintain an upright, if not slightly forward position. Your shoulders should then be relaxed and neutral, as opposed to rigid or hunched. You should be able to maintain this good posture in your sea kayak without a high level of muscle tension. Your muscles (particularly the core muscles) should be in a state of readiness rather than extremely tense or too relaxed; this allows your body to react quickly to changes or demands. If you imagine that you have a piece of string attached to the top of your head constantly pulling you up towards the sky, your posture will be about right.

Connectivity

Connectivity points within the sea kayak.

It is essential that you feel that you are wearing your sea kayak, as opposed to sitting in it. This appropriate connectivity will also allow you to maintain good posture. As with the clothes that you wear, your kayak fit needs to be comfortable and functional as opposed to tight and restrictive or loose and cumbersome. Think about forming a diamond shape of comfortably connected parts of your body within the sea kayak. This diamond shape should be made up of your feet on the foot rests and your back on the back rest as the two ends of the diamond, and then your knees/thighs (depending on boat design) braced on the thigh grips at each side of the diamond. Within this diamond your connectivity through the seat and hips is also important to help drive the boat in the direction you want it to go.

Power transfer

While performing any paddling skill that is moving the sea kayak you should be able to generate positive power transfer. This power transfer is the way you drive the kayak through the water, transferring the pressure from the blade through the body to maximise the power to move the kayak in any given direction. Power transfer is dependent on good posture and connectivity.

Efficient power transfer should ensure that no energy is lost from the system i.e. energy in = movement out. This will usually be done by opposing the pressure on the blade by pushing on the feet or other main contact points within the boat. This in turn transfers the power through the body's core strength. In each skill you perform you will need to be aware of this power transfer so that you use the appropriate connectivity and core muscles.

Feel

It is clear that the above three 'foundation skills' are all inter-related; if we are fully aware of our posture, connectivity and power transfer in all skills, we should also be able to 'feel' what is happening when we are performing in our sea kayak. Developing our feel is all about accepting feedback through our body, the blade, the boat, the water and the environment around us. We can then use this information to anticipate and make adjustments accordingly. It is this 'feel' that allows skills to be performed naturally in all environments, no matter how changeable that environment is. This allows us to work with the water and not fight it.

These fundamentals are often referred to within the skills described throughout this book. They form the solid foundations to all the skills, so when out there practising be sure that your foundations are solid!

LONG-TERM PADDLER DEVELOPMENT

Since 2004, paddlesport has adopted an ethos that is known as long-term paddler development. This involves introducing paddlesport to young and old alike in such a way that they develop their personal skills to the highest level possible, ensuring that it is done in a lifelong sustainable way. In researching how this is best done for paddlers, the above key fundamental concepts have been identified.

3 FORWARD PADDLING

Ninety-nine percent of your time sitting in your sea kayak will be spent paddling forward. It is therefore fair to say that this has got to be the most important skill that we learn. It is also the skill in which you will see the greatest amount of variance between paddlers and the greatest need for improvement.

We will focus on the two most recognised forms of forward paddling technique used on the sea. I would encourage any paddler to develop the ability to perform both of them well in a variety of conditions, and be able to choose between them and adapt them appropriately.

High angle forward paddling

This is the most efficient forward paddling style. It will give you maximum speed in your sea kayak and, when done well, will maximise the use of your larger body muscle groups. However, it requires good posture and appropriately conditioned muscle groups for a paddler to be comfortable paddling day in day out using this style. It also requires good balance in the sea kayak and good body rotation for the stroke to be maintained.

High angle forward paddling.

(Right detail)
relaxed top hand.

catch phase

- Body posture upright with no forward bobbing.

- Arm extended for maximum reach.

- Relax the top hand to prevent wrist strain, improve circulation and reach.

- Maximum reach gained through good rotation.

- Paddle entering water cleanly and near vertical, 'like spearing a fish'.

- Power put on paddle immediately.

power phase

- Unwind rotation of body for power.

Consider taking
you knees out of
the thigh grips and
having legs together
in kayak cockpit.

- Push on foot the same side as paddle blade for power transfer through core muscles.

- Have knees/thighs relaxed in kayak to allow power transfer.

- Paddle stays at a high angle so that the blade tracks near vertically alongside the kayak.

- Paddle is held away from body throughout to maximise rotation.

- Top hand guides and pushes paddle to prepare for next catch phase and stays about level with eyes or just above.

blade exit

- Blade exits at or just before hip.

- As blade exits it is sliced out with no scooping of water.

- Top hand is high and body is in position for final rotation for the next catch.

starting the next catch phase

- Top hand maintains a relaxed grip throughout to maximise reach and prevent wrist strain.

- Top hand is ready for the next catch phase.

- The body is set up in a rotated position.

Low angle forward paddling

This is the forward paddling style that many paddlers use for long distance cruising. It keeps the kayak ticking over at a regular speed. It requires less balance and rotation and uses different muscle groups so can therefore can be sustained longer by many kayakers, as well as feeling more stable. However, it does not move the kayak through the water as effectively, and is not ideal for acceleration or increasing speed or power when forward paddling.

(Right detail) body rotation in catch phase.

catch phase

- Body fairly rotated and blade enters the water at a comfortable reach.

- Blade enters the water at a more horizontal angle (compared to high angle forward paddling).

- Power is applied gradually to paddle.

- Power gained gradually through unwinding the body's rotation.

- Power transfer through pushing on foot nearest the paddle blade.

Consider taking you knees out of the thigh grips and having legs together in kayak cockpit.

- Have knees/thighs relaxed in kayak to allow power transfer.

- Blade follows a wider, more sweeping, track though the water.

- Top hand guides and pushes the paddle to prepare for the next catch phase; paddle shaft stays at about stomach to chest level.

blade exit

- Blade exits just behind the hip.
- Blade exits the water as cleanly as possible without scooping water.
- Top hand remains relaxed on the paddle grip to prevent wrist strain.
- As blade exits, top hand is ready for the next catch phase.

starting new catch phase

- Top hand is ready for the next catch phase.
- The body is set up in a rotated position.

ENVIRONMENT CONSIDERATIONS

The low angle forward paddling stroke can give more support and feel more stable in rougher water, as the paddle takes a more sweeping motion. As the paddle is lower it also catches less wind and will therefore be less affected in high winds. However, it will be a compromise if you need a lot of power to paddle against the wind to get home!

You might, for example, choose to use low angle forward paddling across the wind to minimise paddle flutter and switch to a high angle forward paddle when you round the point and have to paddle into the wind. Paddle flutter is reduced when paddling into wind with feathered blades. Paddling into a strong wind requires more power.

TOP TIPS

Many kayakers will hold their paddle too close when performing strokes, preventing full rotation and control. Pretend you have a beach ball between you and your paddle to avoid your paddle coming too close. You should be able to see your spray deck the majority of the time without your paddle shaft covering it.

When paddling on long journeys, consider swapping between high angle and low angle forward paddling. This rests the different muscle groups as well as maintaining 'perfect practice' in both styles.

EQUIPMENT CONSIDERATIONS

Along with the kayak, the most important piece of equipment for forward paddling and all skills is the paddle. You will need a certain style of paddle depending on your preferred forward paddling style. Alternatively, if you want to be able to paddle in all styles, you will need a paddle which has characteristics of both.

Some top tips include the following, which should all be considered with your own size and strength. For high angle paddling, you will need a shorter length paddle (206–216cm) with a larger asymmetric or 'kinetic' blade. For low angle paddling, a longer paddle (212–222cm) and a smaller or longer blade is needed. Cranked shafts can give power benefits to both styles (and reduce the strain on your wrists). Paddles which vary in length and feather are available, which can provide the perfect tool for the job every time you are out.

4 TRAVELLING IN A STRAIGHT LINE

Although the sea kayak is designed to travel in a straight line with reasonable ease, it also needs to be able to turn and be relatively stable. The compromise between these three design criteria will make it almost impossible to get a 'perfect' sea kayak for everything.

Your sea kayak may not always go in as straight a line as you wish. It will often be the environment that is the root cause of the problem, in particular the wind. There are however some key skills that the paddler can employ to help their kayak travel in a straight line in a variety of conditions.

ENVIRONMENTAL CONSIDERATIONS

The anchored bow as it cuts through the water with the 'looser' water in the 'V' behind.

Left to their own devices, sea kayaks will generally 'head to wind'. This is because the bow of the kayak is anchored as it cuts through the water when moving forward. The stern, however, is less anchored in the disturbed water at the back of the kayak and is therefore 'looser' in the water. Due to this, the stern of the kayak can be blown downwind.

(Left) packing the weight in the stern of a sea kayak. (Centre) a stern-trimmed sea kayak.

(Right) a bow-trimmed sea kayak

Trim

The way in which you pack you kayak will have an effect on how your boat handles. In general, it is best to have a kayak evenly loaded. This way the kayak will have a neutral trim and perform well in most conditions. In windier conditions, the stern of the kayak is generally blown downwind and the kayak goes 'head to wind'. If this is happening to your sea kayak too much, you should consider packing more weight towards the stern of the kayak. This will anchor the stern more or make the skeg/rudder more effective. Alternatively, if your bow is being blown downwind (less common) consider packing more weight in the front so that the boat is trimmed bow heavy.

Edge

Edging into the wind.

As you will read in Chapter 6 you can control and turn a sea kayak very effectively by edging the kayak while paddling. This key skill can also be used to stop a boat turning.

In windy conditions, your kayak will usually 'head to wind'. You can set your kayak on a edge towards the wind to counteract this effect. To comfortably maintain this kind of edge over a long distance, you may want to consider adjusting your seating position by moving your backside to one side of the seat or unweighting one buttock. This maintains the edge through bodyweight (see Chapter 6).

TOP TIP

Try this exercise – sit upright in your kayak, close your eyes and imagine that a painful boil has erupted on your right buttock. Now open your eyes. If your imagination has kicked in you will find that you have unweighted the buttock with the imaginary boil and transferred most of your weight to the other (left) buttock. Your boat will be tilted onto its right edge.

*Pressure applied on the right
foot to help turn the kayak to
the left.*

⇨ *wind direction.*

➡ *foot pressure.*

➡ *foot pressure turns
boat to the left to counteract
the effect of the wind.*

Foot pressure

Alternate foot pressure is an important part of forward paddling.
If you are heading off in one direction more than another you
can apply more foot pressure to compensate. To make this as
effective as possible, try applying increased foot pressure on one
foot only. The pressure should be applied to the opposite foot to
the direction you want to turn your kayak in. For example, if your
kayak is turning to the right, apply constant pressure on your right
foot to bring the kayak back to the left.

Paddle shuffling

Extended paddle grip.

This is another way to correct your kayak in order to maintain a
straight line. Simply shuffle your handgrip along your paddle shaft
so that you have a longer section of paddle in the water on one
side compared to the other. If you then continue forward paddling,
the increased leverage on one side will turn your kayak in the
direction away from the extended paddle side. (This makes your
forward paddling less effective, so use edging and foot pressure
as much as possible and shuffle as little as possible.)

Keyhole stroke

This is a modified forward paddle stroke where instead of the blade finishing at about the hips as previously described, it continues in the water to make corrections to the direction the kayak is travelling in. If the bow of the kayak is turning upwind then a keyhole stroke on the windward side will help correct this. The keyhole stroke works best with a high angle forward paddle stroke.

The forward paddling catch and power phases.

standard catch & power phase

Paddle slicing away keyhole stroke phase.

- Where the paddle blade would usually be lifted out of the water, slice it away and back from the boat.

- Ensure during this slicing phase no pressure is felt on the blade.

- The top hand moving further across the the kayak will help this.

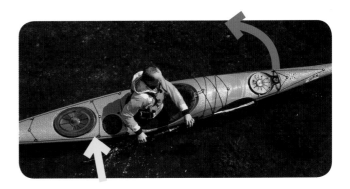

The stern draw part of the keyhole stroke to change the direction of the kayak.
Blade draws toward kayak.
Boat swings to the left.

- The paddle blade is now away from the boat and in a position behind the hip of the paddler.

- The blade is pulled towards the stern of the boat in a stern draw; this turns the kayak bow away from the paddle.

- This uses some rotation.

- The top hand pushing across the front deck of the kayak generates most of the power.

- The kayak is edged towards the paddle blade.

- The paddler remains looking where they are going.

- The paddle is removed from the water just before it touches the stern of the kayak.

- Both hands are now over the edge of the boat.

- The next forward stroke on the opposite side can now follow.

Rudders and skegs

Rudders and skegs are important tools for keeping your kayak travelling in a straight line. There are definite advantages and disadvantages of using rudders or skegs, as well as a certain amount of skill required to use them effectively. For more information on how to use rudders or skegs, see Chapters 12 and 13.

5 REVERSE PADDLING

Whether you are reversing out of a narrow cave you have just explored or launching from a stony beach backwards to save the stones jamming your skeg box, reverse paddling is a key skill for the sea kayaker. As well as being used to move the kayak backwards under control, reverse paddling can also be used to slow down or stop a kayak moving forwards. The skills are very similar for all of the above; they are simply applied with varying amounts of power. When developing your backwards paddling it may seem a little strange at first. This is due to you not seeing where you are going and therefore having less familiar feedback from one of your main senses. Being able to reverse paddle with maximum efficiency takes far more awareness of the 'feel' of the paddle and boat. This is a great sense to develop for all strokes and it is good to develop the 'feel' of all our kayaking skills as much as what they 'look' like.

(Right) body rotation in catch phase.

catch phase

- Maintain good upright posture.

- Rotate body to initiate catch phase.

- Place blade in the water just behind the hips.

- Use the back of the blade to power the kayak backwards.

- Try and plant the blade in the water with as little splash as possible.

- The top hand will be across the deck of the kayak to allow this.

- Knees should not be braced in the kayaks thigh grips but relaxed, allowing power to go directly to the footrests.

power phase

- As soon as blade is fully submerged at hip level, push powerfully with lower hand.

- Use core muscles to help unwind the rotated body.

- Ensure the blade stays parallel with the kayak as close as possible.

- Use top hand to help guide this while pulling gently with it.

- Ensure paddle is held away from the body as with forward paddling.

- To fully engage core muscles, push with foot on the opposite side to the paddle blade.

- Apply maximum power when blade is most vertical between the hips and knees.

blade exit

- Allow blade to exit the water between the knees and feet.

- Use this end of stroke rotation to start the next stroke on the opposite side.

- Consider looking over your shoulder at this stage to check where you are going.

starting the next catch phase

- As the blade exits, the body should already be rotated for the new catch phase.

- Looking over the shoulder on the same side as the new stroke will also aid rotation, but is not required on every stroke (only when you need to check where you are going).

- Through the entire stroke keep the kayak running as balanced and level as possible.

Reversing in a straight line

Here are some pointers to help you with this.

- Whenever possible, paddle with gradual maintained power so that corrections, when needed, are not too great.

- Develop the 'feel' to notice the kayak going offline as soon as it starts to happen.

- If the kayak starts to go offline, use a more sweeping reverse stroke to correct. This can be initiated further back then the normal reverse stroke, similar to the reverse sweep shown in Chapter 7.

- If using a corrective sweep stroke, apply power at the start and finish of this stroke as opposed to the middle part of the stroke.

- When applying a sweep stroke, edge the kayak gently towards the paddle.

- Although not ideal (as it slows or stops the kayak), the kayak can be corrected by applying a forward initiation stroke on the opposite side to the reverse sweep/power stroke.

- It is easier to maintain a straight course while reverse paddling downwind or upwind than across the wind.

TOP TIPS

Try paddling forwards with your eyes closed to develop the 'feel' of keeping the kayak travelling in a straight line. Start paddling backwards, gently at first, eyes closed to get a similar 'feel' for reverse paddling with equal technique and power on both sides.

To help rotation when initiating the catch phase, think about keeping the paddle shaft parallel to your shoulders.

6 EDGING

All sea kayaks, to a greater or lesser degree, are designed for journeying. With this being their main use, it comes as no surprise that the sea kayak is more challenging to manoeuvre than its whitewater or surf counterparts. A skilled sea kayaker will, however, be able to turn their kayak (despite the straight running hull design) in relatively tight spaces with reasonable ease.

There are many ways in which we can turn our sea kayaks and we will explore these in the following chapters. There is however one key skill that underlies all sea kayak manoeuvring and needs to be mastered. This skill is balancing the sea kayak comfortably when it is held at varying degrees of edge to one side or the other.

1 Small amount of edge:

- Good posture is essential to maintain balance; keeping the upper body slightly forward will help.

- Connectivity is needed; with pressure able to be applied and felt on the footrests, thigh grips and backrest.

- Apply gentle pressure on the up-edge knee (left knee in image). Depending on the thigh grips of the sea kayak, the pressure may not be applied by the knee but by the muscle just inside the knee.

- Apply gentle pressure on the down-edge foot (right foot in image).

- A small amount of edge can also be applied by unweighting one buttock; this is good for extended periods of edging (see Chapter 4).

- Keep the head over the centre line of the kayak.

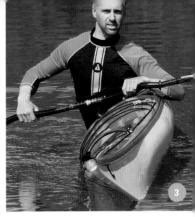

(Above) varying degrees of edge.

2 Medium amount of edge:

- Apply increased pressure on the up-edge knee.

- Apply increased pressure on the down-edge foot.

- Try and maintain constant pressure; use core muscles to help.

- By keeping the head over the centre line of the kayak you may feel 'an inch being pinched' just above your hips (left side in the image).

- Keep a relaxed grip on the paddle; this relaxes the upper body and helps balance.

- Hold the paddle slightly away from the body.

- Maintain good posture, slightly forward.

Body position in relation to edge.

3 Maximum amount of edge:

- A lot of pressure will need to be applied to up-edge knee and down-edge foot; this 'locks' the kayak in position.

- Moving the upper body slightly further forward may help.

- Keeping the head over the centre line is essential.

- Maintain a relaxed grip on the paddle, but resting it in the water for support if needed, can give extra confidence.

- Use the down-edge 'butt cheek' to help monitor and maintain edge pressure.

- Use core muscles to help maintain this edge.

EQUIPMENT CONSIDERATIONS

Depending on the shape of your kayak hull ('V'-chined or rounded) your kayak will edge differently. Many will have secondary stability built in at about a medium edge to make it easy to balance. (Initial stability is when the kayak is upright i.e. its natural balance point.) Find the secondary stability in your kayak so you can use it to best effect. Ensure you have good thigh grips in your kayak so that you can maintain good pressure. For many sea kayaks, you may need to add some foam to the built-in thigh grips and to the hip area, making them more effective and customised for you. If the kayak has a too big a cockpit for you it may be impossible to edge, so ensure you use a kayak that you can wear like a comfortable glove.

TOP TIPS

When starting to edge, practise in a shallow area where you have no concerns about 'over edging'. Number your small, medium and maximum edges 1, 2 and 3 and practice going from flat (0) through 1, 2, 3 and 3, 2, 1 edges on one side and then the other. At each numbered edge, hold for a short period of time initially then gradually build up this time. Experiment doing this with eyes closed, no paddles, body further forward or back and on the move as well as static. To help check that your head is over the centre line, look down occasionally and you should see only your spray deck. Also try holding your kayak paddle out in front of you, level with your eye line and the horizon line, to get your body in the right position.

7 STATIC TURNING

When moving forwards in a straight line, the sea kayak cuts through the water effortlessly. However, when static and needing to change direction, the sea kayak can be a challenging craft to turn. It is therefore essential to blend the good edging skills already discussed with other techniques to help us turn as effectively as possible.

Forward sweep

The forward sweep stoke is the bread and butter turning stroke. Whether you are static or moving and what other strokes you will combine it with, the forward sweep has a few variations. We will explore these as we progress through the book. Here we'll look at its most fundamental form: when the kayak is static and you just want to move the bow of the kayak to the left or right.

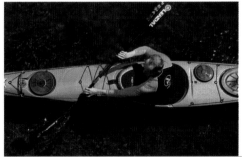

(Right) blade angle used to gain support while edging during the sweep stroke.

sweep initiation

- Rotate upper body.

- Reach forward and plant paddle as far forward as is comfortable. This should be done by body rotation and not by leaning too far forward.

- Looking where you want to go can help this initial rotation.

- Put the kayak on edge towards the paddle blade.

- Apply gentle pressure on the foot nearest the paddle blade for support.

  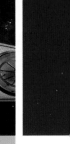

initial power phase

- This first half of the sweep is the most important and is therefore when maximum power should be applied, particularly at the start.

- Unwind upper torso to engage core muscles.

- Looking where you want to go at this initial stage can help engage the core muscles.

- Push hard on the foot nearest the blade, as this is important to help with the power transfer.

- Hold the kayak edged as much as you comfortably can.

- Sweep the paddle in an arc at arms length from the kayak.

- Hold the paddle away from the body in a relaxed position.

- To help balance the kayak on an edge, angle the blade slightly towards the back of the kayak to get some support from the front (power face) of the blade.

- Maintain pressure on blade-side foot and up-edge knee for balance.

- Continue good rotation to finish stroke as near to the stern of the kayak as you feel comfortable.

- Try and keep your chest in line with the paddle shaft to help rotation at the end of the stroke.

- Allow the entire paddle to move out over the water on the sweep side to help finish the stroke.

- Keep blade submerged throughout the stroke.

- Maintain an edge on the kayak.

Reverse sweep

This stroke is essentially the opposite of the forward sweep. Again, it can be used to great effect in combination with other static and moving strokes. It may be used on its own where obstacles make it easier to move the stern rather than the bow.

(Right) blade angle used to gain support while edging during the sweep stroke.

reverse sweep initiation

- Rotate the upper body fully.

- Plant the blade as near to the stern of the kayak as is possible.

- Looking at where you want to place the blade will help rotation.

- Start edging the kayak towards the blade.

- Maintain constant pressure on both feet.

- Angle the back (reverse face) of the blade slightly towards the front of the kayak and it will give some support.

initial power phase

- This first half of the sweep is the most important and maximum power should be applied using the back of the blade, particularly at the start.

- Maintain as much edge as is comfortable.

- Sweep the blade in an arc at arm's length from the kayak.

- Unwind the body rotation to engage the core muscles.

- Pushing hard on the foot away from the blade is important as it helps with power transfer.

final phase of reverse sweep

- Maintain edge on kayak.

- Continue body rotation towards the front of the kayak.

- Keep blade submerged throughout to maintain power.

- Keep pressure on feet and knees to help maintain power and stability.

- Remove the blade from the water as far forward as is comfortable before it touches the kayak.

360° static turns – changing edge

This involves combining the forward and the reverse sweep strokes described above. When the kayak is static, this is the fastest and most efficient way to turn the kayak further than one stroke can. It requires good timing, dynamic edge change, commitment to the edge and good power transfer.

1. Initiation – perform this part of the stroke as described in the forward sweep stroke initiation and power phase.

2. Sweep finish – perform this part of the stroke as described in the forward sweep final phase and finish.

- While the kayak is still turning and the blade is being removed from the water, start to look in the direction you are turning to line up the edge change and reverse sweep initiation.

3. Edge change and reverse sweep initiation – while the kayak is still turning, fully rotate body dynamically to the reverse sweep initiation position.

- At the same time, quickly change edge so you are committed to the reverse sweep edge.

Blade angle to help commit to new edge.

● Have the back of the blade angled towards the front of the kayak at this initiation phase, providing support while committing to the new edge.

● The above should all be happening simultaneously and the reverse sweep initiation and power phase, as already described, should start in one flowing movement.

4 Reverse sweep finish – to continue turning the kayak, repeat the flowing dynamic edge and sweep change back to another forward sweep.

● This change to another forward sweep should be carried out before the kayak stops turning, as with the previous edge change.

● Continue this sequence until the kayak has turned to where you want to be.

360° static turns – on the same edge

Some kayakers find the dynamic edge transfer described above a challenging and unstable man-oeuvre. If this is the case, it may be more effective to turn the kayak without changing edge. This technique is also a more effective way of turning certain designs of sea kayak (for example, those with a very pronounced keel, modified stern or skeg in down position).

1 Initiation – perform this part of the stroke as described in the forward sweep stroke initiation and power phase.

2 Sweep finish – this part of the stroke is the same as the forward sweep final phase and finish.

● Start looking towards the direction you are turning to help initiate the body rotation required for the reverse sweep initiation.

● Maintain constant pressure on feet and knees to maintain the kayak on the same edge while moving to the reverse sweep position.

● This maintained edge is essential and should allow the kayak to continue turning under its own momentum.

3. Same edge reverse sweep initiation – maintain foot and knee pressure to allow blade to be placed in the water.

• Good rotation and flexibility help here to place the blade as near to the stern of the kayak as is comfortable.

• There is no need to angle the back of the blade for support as with previous sweeps.

• Perform the sweep stroke as has already been described, but maintaining the constant edge away from the blade.

4. Reverse sweep finish – the reverse sweep should be finished as already described.

• If further turning is required, maintain the kayak constant edge and initiate another forward sweep stroke sequence.

Extended paddle turns

With all the above turns, the paddle is acting as a lever to turn the kayak. A simple way of making these turns even more effective is to extend the length of this lever. By altering your grip of the paddle and moving your hands nearer one of the blades you will be able to get much more leverage with the paddle, and even tighter turns for less effort. This is easy with the forward or reverse sweep strokes on their own but can be more challenging (even counterproductive) with the 360° turns where you are quickly changing from one sweep to another.

Extended paddle for sweep stroke turn.

ENVIRONMENT CONSIDERATIONS

With all of the above turns, you may find that as the conditions get rougher some of the techniques will work better for you than others. Some sea kayakers may find that the 360° same edge turn works most efficiently for them in calm conditions; they may find it unstable in the rough. In this case, using the changing edge turn may work better. Make sure you know what works best for you in the conditions you are out in, and do not be afraid to change technique to match the conditions. When turning in rougher conditions use the waves to help you by turning on the top of them. This frees the bow and stern from the water and makes turning easier.

EQUIPMENT CONSIDERATIONS

As already mentioned, the hull design of your kayak has an effect on which of the above turns are most efficient for you. The more 'V'-like your keel, the more you will have to experiment to discover which works best; it may well be same edge turns.

TOP TIPS

Good flexibility and core strength will help all of these turns.

To discover which of the 360° turns is most effective for you in your kayak during different conditions is a challenge. To help, choose a marker that the bow of your kayak is lined up with at the start of the turning sequence. Carry out your 360° turn changing edge and count how many strokes it takes to get the bow of your kayak back to the marker. Carry out the same exercise staying on the same edge, and see if it has taken more or fewer strokes. This should help you discover which stroke is most effective. Perhaps try it with your eyes closed so you can feel if you are using similar effort for each method. For this you may need a companion to be the marker and count for you as you'll have your eyes closed!

8 FORWARD TURNS ON THE MOVE

For a sea kayaker to become proficient at exploring the world's coastlines it is essential that they have a variety of methods with which to manoeuvre their kayak. Whether it is moving in and out of rocks or turning the kayak so it is facing downwind when out on the open sea, being able to choose and perform the best technique is essential for success.

There are a number of different methods we can use to turn our moving sea kayak. As well as looking at how to perform these turns, we will also look at when the particular turn will be of most use. This is dependent on sea state, wind conditions, kayaking speeds and the ability of the paddlers.

Edged turning

As we continue to explore how to skilfully paddle our sea kayak, we will also continue to realise how amazing the hull designs are. Once it is up and running at speed, the simple skill of applying a balanced and maintained edge will in itself cause the sea kayak to turn. This edged turn is the most effective and efficient turn we can use on the move, as it uses the hull design to turn the kayak and needs no extra help from the paddler. It is ideally suited for calmer conditions when minimum effort is required and the turn does not need to be too tight. In windy conditions, this turn will not work very well without some assistance from the paddle.

The edged turn on the move. Lifting the right knee will turn the kayak right.

- Ensure that the kayak is moving forward at a reasonable speed.

- Apply and maintain a balanced medium edge to the kayak (see Chapter 6).

- More or less edge can be used to control how tightly the kayak turns.

TOP TIPS

For the majority of sea kayaks, the kayak will turn away from the side it is edged (outside edge) so:

Left knee up – turn left
Right knee up – turn right

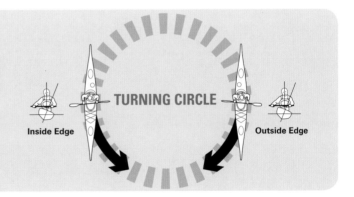

Inside Edge   TURNING CIRCLE   Outside Edge

- To help the kayak turn on this edge, ensure that the last forward paddle stroke is on the side which you edge towards (on the left side in the picture).

- Look towards the direction the kayak is turning.

- The outside paddle blade can be held just above the water to act as a 'stand by' stabiliser. This can give you the confidence to maintain the edge but must not drag and slow the turn.

- You can also keep forward paddling while applying the edge and the kayak will gradually turn without losing forward speed.

Different sea kayaks will turn better on different degrees of edge depending in particular on the waterline on the back deck. It is therefore essential to experiment when turning your kayak on the outside edge. Too extreme an edge may stall the turn with the water pushing on the back deck; a small or medium edge may be more effective in this case.

Occasionally with some very round-hulled kayaks or a low volume/heavily laden kayak it may be easier to turn on the inside edge of the kayak. This is carried out as described above, but using the inside paddle blade as the emergency stabiliser and the final paddle stroke being on the side from which you edge away. You will find that what is shown in the picture will work best the majority of the time, but experiment to see what is suited to your kayak.

Sweep edged turn

Although the edged turn is the most efficient turn as it uses purely the hull of the kayak to effect the turn, there are many times when we may wish to have more control over how tightly we turn the kayak. You may also find that in slightly windier and rougher conditions that edging alone will not turn the kayak. If you need to turn the kayak tighter with more stability in slightly stronger winds and rougher conditions, the sweep edged turn is more efficient.

1 Sweep edged turn initiation – the turn can be initiated while the kayak is on the move or as a way to get the kayak moving.

● Apply a balanced medium or more edge as described in Chapter 6.

● Rotate your body so that it is facing towards the direction you are turning.

● Plant your paddle for a forward sweep initiation as described in Chapter 7.

2 Sweep edged turn finish – apply a powerful half sweep stroke.

● Maintain balanced edge with up-edge knee while driving powerfully with the lower foot on the same side as the paddle blade in the water.

● Keep looking in the direction that the kayak is turning.

● It may be easier to apply power and maintain balance with the body leaning slightly forwards.

- Angle the front of the blade in the water slightly towards the stern of the kayak for support.

- Finish the sweep stroke at the hips when it has had maximum effect and it is still easy to balance the kayak on its optimum edge.

3 + 4 Sweep edged turn recovery – maintain a constant edge throughout the recovery phase so that the kayak continues to turn.

- Move the paddle back to the sweep initiation position, ensuring the upper body is fully rotated.

- Skim the back of the blade across the water so it is available as an emergency stabiliser.

- This blade must not stall the kayak turning, but purely help maintain a constant edge.

- Keep looking in the direction of the turn.

- Keep pressure on the up-edge knee and feet and more pressure on the lower foot that is nearest the sweeping blade.

- Initiate another sweep edged turn and continue until the kayak has turned to its new heading.

Stern draw

The sweep edged turn relies on a good edge and a powerful half sweep to drive the bow of the
kayak around the turn. With reasonable rotation, it can be easier to turn by moving the stern of the
kayak instead of the bow. This is because the stern of the kayak is 'looser'; it is not as fixed by the
water as the bow when cutting through water on the move. The stern draw on the move can be a
more energy-efficient turning stroke when turning the kayak in not too tight a turn, particularly if the
kayak is heavily laden or in moderate winds. The stern draw relies on slightly less rotation and more
arm strength than the final rear part of a static sweep stroke. Many paddlers will find less rotation
easier to perform and more stable when on the move. In their case, the stern draw is therefore
preferred to the final part of a sweep stroke to turn the stern of the kayak on the move.

1. Stern draw initiation – the stern draw can be initiated at the end of
   a forward paddling stroke (see the keyhole stroke in Chapter 4), or
   used repeatedly on its own.

- Rotate the upper body so that the paddle can be held with both
  hands over the water.

- Place the blade in the water a relaxed arms length away from the
  kayak behind the hips.

- Keep facing in the direction of travel.

- Start to edge the kayak towards the blade as much as can be
  balanced comfortably.

- Start to apply pressure on the foot nearest the drawing blade.

  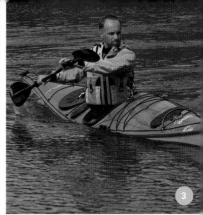

2 Stern draw power phase – Maintain the kayak on a comfortable edge towards the stern draw.

● Keep looking towards the direction of travel.

● Keep blade submerged and pull it towards the stern of the kayak.

● Do this by rotating the body as well as pushing the front hand across the body out over the water and pulling with the rear hand to draw the blade in towards the stern of the kayak.

● The top hand will be at about chest height to allow the above to happen comfortably.

● Apply gentle pressure on the foot on the same side as the stern draw.

2 Blade removal at end of the stern draw – remove the blade from the water just before it touches the side of the kayak towards the stern.

● If further turning is required, place the blade back in the stern draw initiation position and repeat the stroke.

● Maintain the edge while returning the blade to the initiation position to keep the kayak turning.

● To help maintain the kayak on a balanced edge when finishing the stroke and moving it to the new initiation position, the blade can be skimmed across the surface in an emergency stabiliser position, similar to the sweep edged turn.

ENVIRONMENTAL CONSIDERATIONS

In windy conditions when the sea is not too rough, the stern draw can work very effectively to turn the kayak upwind. This is due to the bow of the kayak being more fixed in position by the water and the stern of the boat naturally wanting to blow downwind. When turning the kayak downwind, the sweep edge turn is more powerful and should be more effective.

Stern draw to turn the kayak upwind.

Sweep edge to turn the kayak downwind.

Braced handbrake turn

The turning strokes on the move described so far have all allowed the kayak to keep moving forward at a reasonable speed while turning. This has given us smooth turns that happen gradually. The braced handbrake turn is a much more dynamic turn which should allow the kayak to turn up to 90° very quickly, but in doing this it slows the sea kayak down to a virtual stop. This turn is great to use when getting the kayak turned quickly is more important then maintaining speed, perhaps when turning the kayak to rescue someone behind you. It is also an essential strong wind and rough water turn. In these conditions, the previously described turns may not have quite enough power in them to drive the nose of the kayak through the wind, or it may be too unstable to balance the kayak on a consistent edge. The braced handbrake turn when performed well can give plenty of power as well as stability to turn the kayak.

- **1** Braced handbrake turn sweep stroke initiation – the kayak must be moving forward with good speed – the faster the better.

- Reach as far forward as is comfortable to place the blade as for a forward sweep stroke initiation (see Chapter 7).

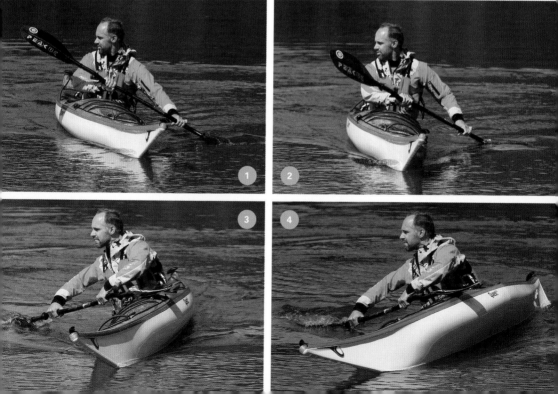

- Ensure that the body is well rotated towards where the kayak is turning and that you are looking in that direction.

- Edge the kayak towards the sweep initiation stroke.

- Apply constant pressure on the up-edge knee and start applying pressure on the foot nearest the sweep initiation stroke.

(2) Braced handbrake turn sweep stroke finish – push powerfully with the foot nearest the sweep stroke.

- Use body rotation to apply power to the blade during the sweep stroke.

- Maintain the kayak on as much edge as is possible.

- Ensure the blade is fully submerged; it can be angled slightly towards the rear of the kayak for increased stability.

- Keep looking towards the direction of the turn.

- Finish the sweep stroke and remove the blade from the water at hip level.

(3) Braced handbrake initiation – at the end of the initiation sweep stroke, before the kayak loses speed, move the blade and place it in a low braced blade position just behind the hips (see Chapter 12 for more on the low braced blade position).

- At the same time, change edge so that the kayak is edged as much as is possible towards the low braced blade.

- Ensure the back of the braced blade is offering support by pushing down on it with constant pressure. Angle the blade slightly up at its front edge so it does not dive in the water.

- To help commit to the edge, hold the braced blade away from the kayak but keep the elbow slightly bent.

- Keep constant pressure on the up-edge knee and feet, with more pressure being applied to the up-edge foot.

Blade angle to brace on.

- The kayak will slow down and start turning around the braced blade.

(4) Braced handbrake turn finish – maintain as much edge as is possible throughout the braced turn.

- To make the turn tighter, move the braced paddle through the water from just behind the hips to near the knees. This is the 'handbrake' part of the turn!

- Use core rotation to move the braced paddle.

- As the kayak comes to a stop, flatten the edge and remove the braced blade from the water.

- If the sea kayak has not turned far enough, you can use the static 360° turn as described in Chapter 7 to finish, as the kayak will be stopped at the end of the braced handbrake turn.

ENVIRONMENTAL CONSIDERATIONS

When turning in rougher water using the braced handbrake turn, timing with the waves can help. Try applying the sweep while riding up a wave so that the braced part can be applied just off the top of the wave. This allows the kayak to turn on the crest of the wave and the momentum off the back of the wave can help the braced part of the turn.

Moving turns are fast but need a lot of space. Static turns take a lot of time but can be performed on the spot. A handbrake turn can be very useful when entering a confined space, precisely because it kills your forward speed.

Bow rudder

The bow rudder can have a similar instant turning effect as the braced handbrake turn. When applied skilfully, it can also give additional control which will allow the paddler to choose by how much the turn will slow down the kayak and exactly how tightly/quickly to turn the kayak. This increased flexibility in the turn comes at a price: stability. In this stroke, the turning blade offers little support and is therefore often used in calmer conditions when more precision and flexibility of turn is needed. Tight manoeuvring among rocks or other obstacles is an example of this.

1. Bow rudder sweep stroke initiation – the bow rudder starts in exactly the same way as the braced handbrake sweep initiation described above.

2. Bow rudder initiation – maintain the kayak on the same edge as with the sweep initiation, i.e. towards the sweeping blade.

Bow rudder blade angle.

- Place the non-sweeping blade into the water vertically on the opposite side to the sweep stroke, about level with the knees.

- The front of the blade should be angled towards your feet.

- The lower arm should be extended in a relaxed and slightly flexed position.

- The top forearm should be across the forehead, this should ensure a vertical paddle blade.

- Bow rudder turning phase – the kayak will start to turn around the vertically placed blade.

- Maintain good body rotation and keep looking in the direction of the turn.

- Maintain as much edge away from the blade in the water as is possible throughout the bow rudder turn.

- Apply increased pressure on the down-edge foot away from the blade in the water.

- Adjust the angle on the blade to change the turn.

- Open the blade up to point more towards the bow of the kayak to increase turn but slow the kayak.

- Close the blade angle up to point more towards the side of the kayak and knees to decrease turn but maintain the speed of the kayak. Keep constant pressure on the blade to help balance the kayak on edge.

4. Bow rudder turning phase finish – by adjusting the angle of the blade you can choose exactly the tightness and speed of turn.

- You can choose to finish the turn when the kayak is pointing where you need to go.

- The bow rudder only works when the kayak is moving forwards, if it slows too much this will also finish the turn.

- If the kayak slows and further turning is still needed you can either use a sweep edged turn or a 360° static turn (see Chapter 7).

TOP TIPS

The key part of the bow rudder is getting the feel of the blade and how it affects the kayak. To get this feel, the blade must be as vertical as possible. It has also been likened to running along and grabbing a pole so you can swing around it: the pole being the blade stuck vertically in the water. To help get the 'feel' of the blade try paddling forwards with the kayak not on edge and just placing the blade vertically at the knees in a bow rudder position. Initially just try and position the blade so it slices through the water with the drive face aligned with the side of the kayak. Gradually open up the blade so that the drive face points more towards the front of the kayak and feel the differences. Try this at slow speeds on both sides to develop this feel and try it with your eyes closed as well as open.

Cross deck bow rudder

The cross deck bow rudder has the same degree of control over the turn as the bow rudder, as well as a similar degree of stability. It is used in very similar situations to the bow rudder. This stroke tends to use more skeletal strength compared to the bow rudder which uses muscular strength, therefore it can be more energy efficient. As well as this, the non-active blade does not move over your head so you will find drips of water do not end up down your neck! As it relies on more skeletal strength, great care must be taken with this stroke if being performed at higher speeds. It also requires more flexibility, co-ordination and balance, and will therefore not suit all kayakers. Many kayakers will end up preferring either the bow rudder or the cross deck bow rudder; they both have their advantages and to be able to perform both is the ideal.

Body and blade position in rudder.

 Cross deck bow rudder sweep stroke initiation – the cross deck bow rudder starts in exactly the same way as the braced handbrake sweep initiation described above.

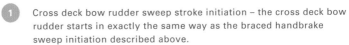 Cross deck bow rudder initiation – maintain the kayak on the same edge as with the sweep stroke initiation i.e. towards the sweeping blade.

- Remove the sweeping blade and move it across the front deck of the kayak.

- Place it vertically in the water about level with your knees.

- The front face of the blade should be angled towards your feet.

- The body should be fully rotated and the lower arm will be fully extended.

- The upper arm should be relaxed holding the shaft as vertical as possible. The elbow should be level with the shoulder and hand.

- The kayak will start to turn around the blade.

3 + **4** Cross deck bow rudder turning phase – maintain as much edge as possible away from the blade in the water throughout the turn.

- Apply increased pressure on the down-edge lower foot away from the paddle.

- As with the bow rudder, the angle of the blade can be adjusted to achieve the desired turn and speed.

- Maintain constant pressure on the blade to help with stability.

- As with the bow rudder, this stroke needs speed for it to work. You can choose when to finish the stroke or it will finish when you do not have enough speed to turn the kayak.

- If further turning is required at the end of the cross deck bow rudder, use either a sweep edge turn or a 360° changing edge static turn (Chapter 7), starting with the reverse sweep on the same side as the rudder.

EQUIPMENT CONSIDERATIONS

When deciding on whether to use a bow rudder or a brace turn, the kayak you paddle can dictate the turn as well as the conditions and type of turn you want. If you have a kayak with a very defined 'V' keel hull, modified stern or you have your skeg down, the bow rudder style turn may be more effective as the keel or skeg is on an edge preventing it digging into the water during the turn. The disadvantage in this is that these turns can be more challenging to balance in rougher conditions. If you are in these types of kayak and prefer the brace turn then the bracing part of the turn will need to be on an extreme edge to get the best effect. This is because the extreme edge will lift the keel, modified hull or skeg further out of the water, thus preventing them from digging in.

It is possible to perform both of the bow rudders by changing onto the inside edge after the initiation sweep stroke. With some boats this may be more effective and it is worth experimenting with. Another consideration is that this may feel more stable in rougher conditions and still be reasonably effective.

9 REVERSE TURNS ON THE MOVE

There are times when we need to turn our kayak in reverse, for example when reversing out of a cave or when launching your kayak in reverse to avoid the skeg getting jammed. Another scenario is that in certain wind and sea conditions it is sometimes easier to turn the kayak in reverse.

Reverse sweep edged turn

This technique is very similar to the forward sweep edged turn and would be used in similar situations e.g. when you need to maintain some backwards speed and the turn can be more gradual as opposed to very tight. This could be when you are reverse paddling and need to slightly alter your course, or when reversing out of a cave where you have plenty of space and need to turn the kayak a small amount as you glide out.

1. Reverse sweep edged turn initiation – fully rotate your upper body as much as is possible.

- Plant the blade as far back and as close to the rear of the kayak as you can.

- Look at where you want to place the blade and behind you; this will help rotation.

- Start edging the kayak towards the blade.

- Have the back of the blade angled slightly towards the front of the kayak for extra support.

- Maintain constant pressure on the up-edge knee and feet, with slightly more on the lower foot.

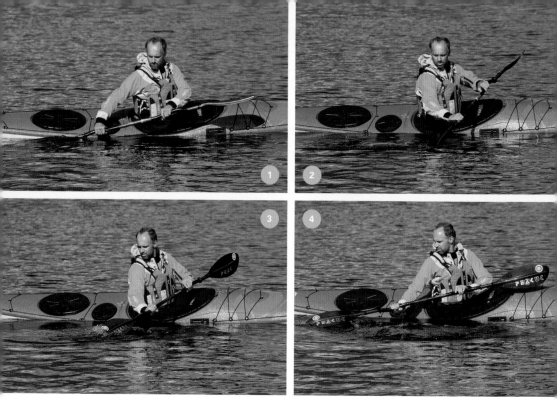

(Sequence) the edged turn on the move.

(2) Reverse sweep edged turn power phase – sweep the blade in an arc away from the back of the kayak.

● Push powerfully on the back of the blade while sweeping.

● Unwind the body rotation to help this.

● Commit to as much edge as feels comfortable; the angled blade should help this.

● Push hard on the upper foot away from the blade to help with the power transfer.

● Finish the reverse sweep stroke when the blade is level with the hips.

(3) + (4) Reverse sweep edged turn blade recovery – as the reverse sweep finishes at the hips, remove the blade from the water.

● Angle the blade with the top edge towards the stern of the kayak. This will allow the front face of the blade to skim across the water as it is returned to the stern of the kayak for another reverse sweep stroke if needed.

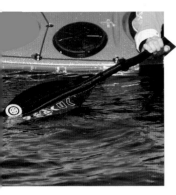

- The top edge of the blade will need to be angled slightly up so it does not dive into the water.

- Maintain the kayak on edge throughout the blade recovery; the skimming blade should offer some support to help with this.

- Ensure that the skimming blade does not have too much pressure on it, which will slow or stall the kayak.

- Maintain constant foot and upper knee pressure.

- Fully rotate the body in order to initiate another reverse sweep stroke to continue the turn.

Angle of recovery of the blade.

Reverse braced handbrake turn

This turn is similar to the forward version in that it is dynamic and will turn the kayak very quickly through a tight angle. In doing this, it will also slow down or stop the kayak from moving in reverse. This turn can be used in calm conditions when a quick effective turn is needed, but it is also the reverse turn of choice in rougher or windier conditions as it provides a surprising amount of stability. In certain windy conditions, this turn can prove to be more effective than any of the forward turns.

- **1** Reverse sweep stroke initiation – the kayak must be moving backwards at a reasonable speed.

- Apply a reverse sweep edged turn initiation as described earlier in this chapter.

- **2** Reverse sweep stroke power phase – apply reverse sweep edged turn power phase.

- Remove the blade from the water vertically when level with hips.

- **3** Reverse braced handbrake initiation – at the end of the reverse sweep initiation stroke, before the kayak loses speed, place the non-reverse sweeping blade in a high brace blade position as far forward as can comfortably be reached on the opposite side to the reverse sweep stroke (see Chapter 12 for more information on high brace position).

- When placing the braced blade, ensure the body is rotated and you are looking in the direction of the turn.

- At the same time, change edge so that the kayak is edged as much as is possible towards the high brace blade.

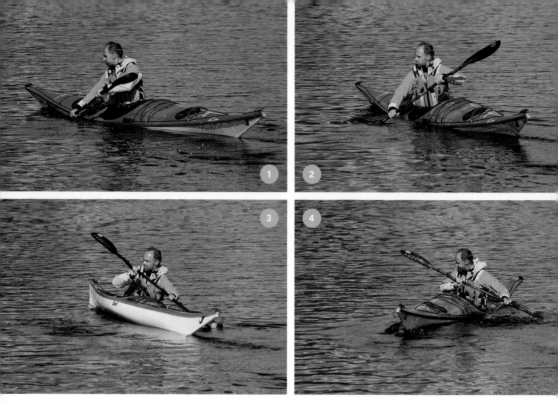

(Sequence) the reverse handbrake turn.

- Ensure the front face of the braced blade is offering support by pulling down on it; angle the top edge of the blade up slightly so it does not dive in the water.

- Keep constant pressure on the up-edge knee and feet, with more pressure being applied to the down-edge foot.

- The kayak will slow down and start turning around the braced blade.

- **4** Reverse braced handbrake turn finish – maintain as much edge as is possible throughout the braced turn.

- To make the turn tighter, move the braced paddle through the water from the bow of the kayak in an arc to about level with the hips; this is the 'handbrake' part of the turn!

- Use core rotation to move the braced paddle and push on the down-edge lower foot for power transfer.

- Continue to look in the direction of the turn.

- As the kayak comes to a stop, flatten the edge and remove the braced blade from the water.

- If the sea kayak has not turned far enough, you will be able to use the static 360° turn. Commit to a reverse sweep stroke on the opposite side and edge, as described in Chapter 7, to finish.

ENVIRONMENTAL CONSIDERATIONS

The reverse braced handbrake turn can work very effectively when turning in strong winds and certain sea states. If you are paddling into the wind or into the swell, it can sometimes be very difficult to generate enough speed to be able to do a forward turn to get the bow of the kayak away from the wind or swell. If this is the case, then go with nature and start paddling in reverse with the wind or swell. With this backwards speed, do a reverse braced handbrake turn.

When the kayak is across the wind and you want to turn downwind, it can be very difficult to turn the bow of the kayak downwind. In this case, try paddling backwards and doing the reverse braced handbrake turn ensuring you turn the rear of the kayak upwind. This will leave you with the nose of the kayak downwind.

The reverse braced handbrake turn is sometimes known as the 'high wind turn'.

10 STERN RUDDERS

Stern rudders are used to keep the kayak going in a straight line and make small directional changes when on the move. The stern rudder only works if the kayak is travelling at a reasonable speed, but it has many applications. The most common is when there is a following wind or sea pushing the kayak along at speed. In this situation, forward sweep strokes are not quick enough to have as much effect as the stern rudder. A similar application is when controlling the kayak while surfing.

A more 'gentle' application is when moving in and out of rocks, caves and arches at slower speeds. Here, the stern rudder provides control and keeps the kayak on course in these tight spaces.

Low angle stern rudder

This is the classic stern rudder and works well to keep the kayak running in a straight line. It is best combined with the push/pull method of turning with a stern rudder (see below).

- The kayak must be moving at a reasonable speed.

- Fully rotate the body so that both hands are out over the side.

- Keep looking forwards.

- Place the blade nearest the stern of the kayak in the water as far back as your rotation allows.

- The blade face should be parallel to the side of the kayak so that it cuts through the water and you feel no resistance.

- The blade should be fully submerged and will act like a rudder, controlling the direction of the kayak.

- The front hand should be across the kayak and at a height between your stomach and chest.

- .Balance the kayak, keeping constant pressure on knees and feet.

High angle stern rudder

The high angle stern rudder has emerged from whitewater paddling, but it also works very well in the sea kayak. With the front hand higher than for the low angle stern rudder, it allows the back blade to be more vertical and deeper in the water. This allows a different range of control and steering methods to work to greater effect, in particular the feathered blade rudder (see below). Another consideration is that some people will find it easier to fully rotate the body when the top hand is higher.

- The kayak must be moving at a reasonable speed.

- Fully rotate the body and place the blade nearest the stern of the kayak in the water as your rotation allows.

- The front hand should be between shoulder and eye height.

- The blade face should still be parallel to the side of the kayak, but it will be more vertical in the water.

- The blade should be fully in the water for maximum control, allowing it to act as a rudder and control the direction of the kayak.

- The upper body can lean back to allow the blade to be placed as near to the rear of the kayak as possible.

- Maintain constant pressure of knees and feet for balance.

Push/pull rudder

Both of the above stern rudders will keep the kayak moving in a straight line. There are occasions when you will need to use the stern rudder to change direction. This could be to avoid a rock when going through an arch or because following wind and waves are pushing the kayak offline. The push/pull rudder can help with this and can be used with the high or low angle stern rudder.

Body rotation and paddle shaft position.

1 Push/pull rudder initiation:

- The kayak must be moving at a reasonable speed.

- Place the blade in a low or high angle stern rudder as described above.

2 Push/pull rudder action:

- To change direction towards the paddle side (the kayaker's right in picture), push the back blade away from the rear of the kayak.

- Keep the front hand in the same position as this acts as the pivot point.

- To change direction away from the paddle side (the kayaker's left in picture), pull the back blade towards the rear of the kayak.

(Below) push/pull rudder, initiation and push.

Feathered blade rudder

The feathered blade rudder allows the kayaker to adjust course with great accuracy in both directions. It allows the kayak direction to be changed equally both towards and away from the paddle side. This gives it an advantage over the push/pull technique. The feathered blade rudder requires good blade awareness in the water and ideally needs to be combined with good use of edge.

1 Feathered away stern rudder initiation – perform a high angle stern rudder as described above.

● Rotate the lower wrist (knuckles down) as if decelerating the throttle on a motorbike, to feel water pressure on the back of the blade, which is now feathered away from the kayak (see picture).

2 The kayak will start to turn towards the paddle side (the kayaker's right in picture).

● The back of the blade can be feathered more or less to increase or decrease the kayak turning.

The feathered away blade angle.

feathered away stern rudder

The feathered towards blade angle.

1 Feathered towards stern rudder initiation – perform a high angle stern rudder as previously described.

● Rotate the lower wrist (knuckles up), as if accelerating the throttle on a motorbike, to feel water pressure on the front of the blade, which is now feathered towards the kayak (see picture).

2 The kayak will start to turn away from the paddle side (the kayaker's left in the picture).

● The front of the blade can be feathered more or less to increase or decrease the kayak turning.

Use of edge

Using the edge of the kayak while it is moving can have a great effect when turning the kayak. By blending edging with the stern rudders we gain far more control over our kayak, particularly when using stern rudders to change direction.

Edge away stern rudder.

- Edge away stern rudder – put the kayak on a comfortable edge away from the paddle side (lifting right knee in picture).

- This on its own will start turning the kayak (right knee up turns kayak right in picture).

- Combine this with the appropriate turning rudder for greater effect. This is either feathering blade away (as in picture), or pushing blade away.

Edge towards stern rudder.

- Edge towards stern rudder – put the kayak on a comfortable edge towards the paddle side (lifting left knee in picture).

- This will start turning the kayak (left knee up turns kayak left in picture).

- Combine this with the appropriate turning rudder for greater effect. This is either feathering blade towards (as in picture) or pulling blade towards.

TOP TIPS:

PUSH/PULL STERN RUDDER	FEATHERED STERN RUDDER	EDGE TURNING (CHAPTER 8)
Edge kayak away – push paddle away	Edge kayak away – feather paddle away	Right knee up – turn right
Edge kayak towards – pull paddle towards.	Edge kayak towards – feather paddle towards	Left knee up – turn left

Bracing stern rudder

In following seas and winds, many paddlers find the stern rudder an unstable stroke. We can modify the stern rudder to give us more stability, yet still have its directional control in a following sea/wind situation. The bracing rudder does slow the kayak down slightly, but this is outweighed by the stability it can give in these conditions.

It is best to develop the skill to perform the stern rudders described above in all conditions. However, although something of a compromise, this is a great 'survival' stroke to use while we develop that skill.

Bracing stern rudder. (Left) the bracing blade angle.

- With the kayak moving, half rotate the upper body.

- Place the blade in a low brace position just behind the hips (see Chapter 12 for more on the low brace blade position).

- Ensure the back of the braced blade is offering support by gently pushing down on it and holding it out from the kayak.

- Angle the blade slightly up at its front edge, so it does not dive in the water.

- At the same time, edge the kayak slightly towards the low braced blade.

- Keep constant pressure on the up-edge knee and feet.

Bracing stern rudder in windy conditions.

- This position can be used to stop the kayak turning. In the picture, the paddler is using the braced stern rudder to stop the kayak turning left.

- Depending on the wind/following sea, place the braced stern rudder on the side that prevents the boat being turned by the conditions.

- A right side braced stern rudder (see picture) will stop the kayak turning left; a left side braced stern rudder will stop the kayak turning right.

EQUIPMENT CONSIDERATIONS

Sea kayaks with more rounded hulls will tend to turn easier. The stern rudder is great for keeping them in a straight line. Use the stern rudder with no edge for this.

Sea kayaks with pronounced 'V'-keeled hulls will tend to stay in a straight line. When using the stern rudder to change direction with these designs, ensure a good edge is combined with the rudder.

ENVIRONMENT CONSIDERATIONS

When using any of the stern rudders to control the direction of the sea kayak in a following sea, consider where best to apply the rudder. Try and time the turn to coincide with the sea kayak on the top half of the following wave; this will make the kayak very responsive and easier to turn. In this situation, less of the stern is in the water and turning is easier. If the sea kayak is on the bottom half of the wave, the stern of the sea kayak will be locked in the wave, preventing easy turning. If the sea kayak is in the trough of the waves, then both the stern and bow may well be locked by the wave behind and in front, preventing any turning.

TOP TIPS

As a practice for stern rudders to ensure that your body rotation is correct, try the following. Lay the paddle floating in the water parallel to the kayak. Reach around and pick up the paddle using both hands in the paddling grip. This is the rotated body position for the stern rudder. Having picked up the paddle, hold it just above the water alongside the kayak. The blade nearest the stern should have its front face towards the kayak. Drop this blade into the water and slice it to the front of the boat. It should feel like you are trying to paddle backwards but with the blade slicing through the water. This is good for rotation and also to get a feel for the paddle blade i.e. whether it is slicing or being feathered and the amount of pressure on it. Try this on your left and right sides, eyes closed, slow and fast.

11 MOVING SIDEWAYS

Moving a five metre long sea kayak sideways is never going to be the easiest of manoeuvres. There are plenty of situations where the kayak may need to be moved sideways, for example: to avoid an obstacle, to raft up next to someone or when approaching a jetty side-on. The following are a range of techniques used to move the kayak sideways when stationary and on the move.

Draw stroke

This stroke is designed to move the kayak sideways when it is stationary in the water. It is what you could use if you wanted to move the kayak closer to someone when rafting up or to make the final adjustments when landing against a jetty. Of the static draw strokes, it is the most powerful and can be used to quickly move the kayak over shorter distances or if needing maximum power to move sideways against the wind.

- Rotate the upper body so that it is facing sideways in the direction the kayak is going to move.

- Ensure you are looking in this direction as well.

- Plant the blade in the water, with the paddle shaft as vertical as possible, a comfortable distance away from the side of the kayak.

- The blade should be roughly in line with your hips, with the front face of the blade towards the side of the kayak (see picture).

*(Right detail) draw stroke
initiation blade angle.*

- The top hand should be stretched out over the side of the kayak, about level with the forehead.

- Edge the kayak towards the paddle.

- Maintain constant pressure on up-edge knee and feet for balance, with slightly more pressure on the lower foot nearest the paddle blade.

draw stroke power phase

- Maintain body rotation and look in the direction of travel throughout.

- Pull the blade directly towards the side of the kayak level with the hips; this should 'draw' the kayak sideways.

- The paddle and blade should be kept as vertical as possible.

- The top hand, as well as the bottom hand, should stay out over the side of the kayak throughout.

- The blade should remain fully submerged.

- Ensure that the kayak is edged towards the paddle for maximum efficiency. This helps prevent the keel digging into the water too much.

- Stop 'drawing' the blade towards the kayak just before it touches the side of the kayak.

(Right detail) draw stroke recovery blade angle.

draw stroke blade recovery

- Keep the blade submerged in the water throughout.

- Maintain body rotation and looking in the direction of travel.

- Maintain edge towards the paddle blade.

- Rotate blade by rolling the wrist, knuckles towards the front of the kayak (as in decelerating the throttle on a motorbike). The front and back face of the blade in the water should now be at 90° to the side of the kayak (see picture).

- Slice the blade away from the kayak at 90° until it is back in the draw stroke initial position.

- Ensure the paddle and blade remain as vertical as possible and that both hands are out over the side of the kayak. This helps to control the slicing blade.

- Rotate the blade back into the draw stroke initiation position and continue the draw stroke sequence.

Sculling draw

The sculling draw is used in similar situations to the draw stroke described above. A difference is that the sculling draw is slightly less powerful and more sustainable. If the kayak needs to be moved sideways a longer distance, the sculling draw is therefore a better choice. A disadvantage is that it may not be powerful enough when moving against a wind.

sculling draw initiation

- Place the blade in the water as far forward as is comfortable between the knees and feet.

- The paddle and blade should be as vertical as is possible in the water.

- The front blade face should be angled so that it is pointing towards the stern of the kayak (see picture).

- The top hand should be reaching out over the side of the kayak about level with the forehead.

- Look in the direction of the sideways movement.

- Edge the kayak towards the paddle blade.

- Maintain pressure on feet and the up-edge knee for balance, with slightly more pressure on the lower foot nearest the paddle blade.

To show the blade angle, the paddle is shown half out of the water. Normally the blade should be fully submerged.

sculling draw blade angle phase 1

finishing phase 1

- Move the vertical paddle towards the back of the kayak parallel with the side of the kayak.

- Keep the blade angle as for the initiation stage, so that constant pressure is felt on it throughout the stroke.

- Rotate the upper body with the paddle blade so that core strength powers the stroke.

- This sustained power on the angled blade should start moving the kayak sideways.

- Keep looking in the direction of sideways movement.

- Maintain a balanced edge towards the paddle blade.

- At the end of the stroke, the paddle should be behind the hips.

(Right detail) Sculling draw blade angle for the second phase. (Blade lifted from water for clarity)

sculling draw blade angle phase 2

finishing phase 2

- When the stroke finishes behind the hips, change the blade angle so that the front face of the blade is angled towards the bow of the kayak (see picture).

- Move the vertical blade towards the bow of the kayak while keeping it parallel to the side, back to the sculling draw initiation position.

- Keep the blade angle constant with the front blade face angled towards the bow of the kayak. Pressure is felt on the blade throughout the stroke.

- Rotate the upper body with the paddle blade so that core strength powers the stroke.

- The constant power on the angled blade should continue moving the kayak sideways.

- Keep looking in the direction of sideways movement.

- Maintain a balanced edge towards the paddle blade.

- Ensure the paddle and blade remain as vertical as possible and that both hands are out over the side of the kayak; this helps control the sculling blade.

- When the blade is back to the sculling initiation position, change the blade angle and continue the sculling draw.

- This vertical sculling motion should be constant and flowing.

- By making slight adjustments to the blade angle, the power of the sculling draw stroke can be altered as well as the direction of travel.

Draw on the move

The draw on the move is a method of moving the kayak sideways quickly and powerfully when travelling forwards. A common use of this stroke would be to avoid a sudden obstacle, such as a rock just under the surface that is not seen until the last minute. This stroke needs to be performed powerfully for maximum effect, as the first drawing motion is what moves the kayak sideways.

1. Draw on the move initiation – with the kayak moving forwards, reach out as far as feels comfortable and place the blade in a draw stroke initiation position.

- Keep the paddle as vertical as is possible.

- Ensure that the entire blade is submerged in the water.

- Start edging the kayak towards the paddle blade.

Blade angle of finish.

2 Draw on the move power phase – draw the blade through the water powerfully towards the kayak, keeping the blade level with hips.

● Edge the kayak as much as is comfortable towards the drawing paddle blade.

● Finish the draw stroke just before the blade touches the kayak side.

3 Draw on the move finish – maintain the 'drawing' blade angle.

● Lift the blade, slicing it out of the water towards the stern of the kayak.

● Maintain both hands out over the side of the kayak to help control the slicing blade.

● Continue paddling forwards, or repeat the process if further sideways movement is needed.

TOP TIPS

When performing the draw on the move, the kayak may not stay in a straight line but veer off to the left or right. If this is the case, as with the draw stroke, try adjusting the position forward or back. Before this, however, ensure that when the blade is placed in the water it is slicing with no resistance. If resistance is felt, the blade will be in a vertical sculling position and this will have a turning effect. While the kayak is moving forwards, practice placing the blade in the draw initiation position. You should feel the blade slicing through the water with no resistance on it; try this on both sides and then with eyes closed as well.

Hanging draw

With the hanging draw, as long as the kayak has forward movement it will continue to be moved sideways. It can move the kayak sideways a lot further than the draw on the move if there is reasonable forward speed. This stroke is less powerful than the draw on the move and will therefore not move the kayak sideways as quickly. It is often used when manoeuvring around rocks and obstacles when the obstacle is seen a little way off, when there is plenty of time to use the stroke to line up the kayak. It can also be used to make fine adjustments to the line of the kayak when moving at relatively low speed through narrow passages and gaps in rocks.

1. Hanging draw initiation – for maximum control of the hanging draw, place the blade on the same side as the last forward stroke taken.

- To place the blade as efficiently as possible, continue the forward stroke towards the stern of the kayak.

- When finishing the extended forward stroke, angle the blade in the water the same as a high angle stern rudder (see Chapter 10).

- Start to angle the blade so that it is slightly feathered away from the kayak.

- While angling the feather on the blade, slice it forwards into the draw stroke initiation position.

- Start edging the kayak towards the paddle blade.

2 + 3 Maintaining the hanging draw – as the blade gets towards the hanging draw position open the blade angle up so the feather angle is similar to the sculling draw.

- Pressure should be felt on the front of the blade and the kayak should move sideways.

- Edge the kayak as much as is comfortable; the more the better.

- Maintain constant pressure on the up-edge knee and feet, with slightly more pressure on the lower foot nearest the paddle blade.

As the blade is sliced into position, you can easily choose the best position as you are slicing. It will usually be somewhere around level with the hips.

- The body should be rotated, but the head is best looking forwards in the direction of travel.

- The final position of the blade should be where the kayak is moving sideways most effectively.

- Maintain the hanging draw position until enough sideways movement has been gained, or the kayak has stopped moving.

- If the kayak has stopped and more sideways movement is needed, then use either the draw stroke or sculling draw.

TOP TIPS

To check your body is in the correct position try the exercise described in coaching top tips at the end of Chapter 10. This time, however, stop the exercise when the paddle shaft is vertical; this will be your draw stroke body position and blade finish position.

All of the draw strokes (particularly the hanging draw) require very good blade awareness. To help with this, try drawing shapes and letters in the water next to you with the blade fully submerged in a draw stroke finish position. When drawing the shapes and letters try to do so with the blade constantly slicing and feeling no pressure on it, holding the paddle shaft as you would when doing a draw stroke. After a few shapes try drawing them faster, slower, bigger, smaller, eyes closed and eyes open, all on both sides.

EQUIPMENT CONSIDERATIONS

The exact position of the draw strokes in relation to the hips, and the amount of feather for a sculling draw, will depend upon the kayak, how it is loaded and the conditions. Practice the draw strokes with your kayak in a variety of conditions, when it is empty and when it is loaded; be prepared to adjust the positions as needed. The degree of edge will also vary depending on how much of a 'V'-keeled hull the kayak has. The greater the level of 'V' hull, the more edge is needed.

12 SUPPORT STROKES

No matter how well we can balance or handle our sea kayak, occasionally we may need that little bit of extra support. This may be because we are trying too hard to get as extreme an edge as possible. Maybe the conditions, such as a sudden gust of wind or an unseen breaking wave, catch us by surprise. As we become confident in our sea kayak we may choose to explore or play in rougher conditions, surf or tidal races. These environments are very changeable and prone to testing your skills unexpectedly. Good support strokes help us to enjoy these places safely.

Low brace

The low brace is the 'bread and butter' support stroke that, in time, should become second nature to the paddler. When this is the case, the moment balance is lost the low brace is there to support the kayak and prevent the situation getting any worse. As well as being a reactive stroke, the low brace is also used as a planned stroke to provide support in anticipation of that 'tippy' moment. For example, if a small breaking wave is coming side on to the kayak, the low brace can be applied onto the top of the wave to provide stability. The brace can also be applied for stability on crossing from slack water into moving water when kayaking in tidal streams. In addition to this, the low brace type stroke can be used in combination with other strokes to help balance on the edge during certain manoeuvres, such as the braced handbrake turn in Chapter 8 and the bracing stern rudder in Chapter 10.

1 Low brace initiation – ensure that upper body posture is upright or slightly forward.

● Place the back of the blade on the water at right angles to the kayak and out to the side: this is the 'braced' position.

● Raise elbow nearest the blade so that it is above the paddle shaft; the elbow should form a right angle.

● The paddle shaft should not be too close to the body but held a small comfortable distance away, still allowing the elbow to be above the paddle.

● Allow the hand and elbow furthest from the blade on the water to hold the paddle in a relaxed manner.

● When practising, or when it is a planned low brace, put the kayak on a balanced edge towards the braced blade.

● If supporting for real, this is the position to instantly get into.

2 Getting support from the low brace – at this stage the kayak is no longer balanced on its edge. To prevent capsize, support is required from the braced blade.

● This will either have happened for real or, if practising, you will have over-edged the kayak out of balance.

● Ensure that the upper body and head stay as upright as possible, over the kayak at all times and not over the water.

● With the elbow at right angles, it will be possible to push directly down on the braced blade for support.

● The hand furthest from the braced blade should maintain a relaxed grip and some support can be gained from resting the paddle shaft on the up edge of the kayak.

3 Using the brace to get back into balance – push fully down on the braced blade.

● At the same time, lift up the down-edge knee and apply instant pressure on it to pull up the kayak into a more level and balanced position.

● As this happens, relax the up-edge knee but apply some pressure on the foot.

● Maintain upright upper body and head. However, if extreme support is required, consider dropping the head towards the water on the side of the bracing blade as the down-edge knee is lifted up.

● A slightly forward body posture will help regain the balance of the kayak.

Angle of recovery
of the blade.

4 Low brace finish – keep applying pressure on the down-edge knee to continue pulling the kayak up to a balanced position.

● As the kayak comes into balance, lower the elbow over the blade and rotate the wrist backwards (knuckles towards you as if accelerating on the throttle of a motorbike) to change the angle on the bracing blade.

● The bracing blade should move to a vertical position with the back of the blade now facing forwards in the water (see picture).

● As you slice blade out of the water there should be no resistance on the blade; this would make the low brace finish very unstable.

When learning the low brace, practise the pushing down on the braced blade and the finish with the kayak level and balanced. When this is done, practise transferring from one edge to the other as fast as you can, but not going to an extreme edge. This will give the feeling of pulling the kayak up with the down-edge knee while maintaining relaxed hips. To bring it all together, gradually edge the boat off balance more and more to get the feel of the low brace; doing this in shallow water or with a partner is good. When the low brace is being performed well, your partner could stand behind you in the water and tip the kayak off balance. This will allow you to react for real in a safe setting.

High brace

The high brace stroke is the stage on from the low brace and is used when the kayak is even more off balance. On calm water this is unlikely, but in swell, surf and rougher conditions the high brace can be useful. If, in extreme conditions, you find yourself trying to lift the paddle shaft higher than your shoulders, it is worth considering capsizing and rolling instead (much better than risking a shoulder dislocation). However, performed well the high brace gives the kayaker that final 'get out of jail free' card.

The term 'high' brace is misleading. Performed safely, the elbows are bent and the shaft of the paddle is kept as low as possible. The real difference is that you push down on the paddle for the low brace and pull down for the high brace.

1. High brace initiation – ensure that upper body posture is slightly forward.

- The front face of the blade should be placed out to the side of the kayak and slightly forward on the water in a braced position.

- The elbow should be lower than the paddle, this will allow the paddle to be pulled down.

- It is essential that the elbow is well bent and not extended, otherwise this stroke can cause injury to the shoulder.

- The kayak will start to edge towards the bracing blade.

- This position needs to be attained instantly if a brace is needed, or got into if practising or expecting the high brace.

2 + 3 + 4 Using the high brace to support and regain balance – the kayak will be a long way off balance.

- Keep the body forward to help with this stroke and protect the shoulders.

- Pull down powerfully on the braced blade, keeping the elbow below the paddle.

- Keep this elbow well bent at all times so that it cannot be over-extended.

- The arm and hand away from the bracing blade should be tucked into the body to support the paddle and protect the shoulder.

- As the braced blade is being pulled down, drive the down-edge knee up powerfully to continue pulling the kayak up to a level balanced position.

- At the same time, release the pressure off the up-edge knee and push with that foot.

- Keep the hips relaxed to allow the above to happen.

Note that in photo 4 the boat rolls back into balance before the body.

- By keeping the hips relaxed, the kayak will be able to move back into a balanced position.

- The kayak should start getting back into a balanced position before the upper body starts to move, the hips acting as a hinge.

- To help get more power from the bracing blade, consider dropping the head towards the water while driving up with the down-edge knee.

5. High brace finish – when the kayak starts to become balanced, maintain pressure on the knees and feet.

- Lift up the elbow and rotate the wrist (roll knuckles away as if decelerating the throttle on a motorbike) on the side of the bracing blade to help change the angle on the blade.

- The bracing blade should move to a vertical position with the back of the blade now facing forwards in the water (see picture).

- The blade should be sliced out of the water with no pressure on it. Moving it slightly backwards as it is sliced can help this.

- Continue to maintain good posture to help finish the high brace and bring the kayak back into balance.

ENVIRONMENTAL CONSIDERATIONS

When out in rougher water such as small to medium waves and surf, anticipate the waves as they are coming side on towards you. At the point they are about to hit the side of the kayak and cause instability, place a low or high brace on top of the wave. At the same time edge the kayak towards the oncoming wave and maintain the brace position. As the wave moves under the kayak you can release the brace and continue in balance. Ensure that you maintain good forward posture and keep your hips relaxed to allow the kayak to move with the wave.

In big surf or breaking waves, do not try to put the blade on top of the wave. Instead, keep the paddle below shoulder height and 'stab' it into the wave. The rotational movement of the water in the wave will provide you with all the support you need without risking a shoulder dislocation. If in doubt … take the roll!

TOP TIPS

When first practising the high brace, consider placing the bracing blade on a partner's boat, a low rock, or even have your partner holding the blade in the water. This will give plenty of support to get the feel of pulling down on the paddle and driving up with the down-edge knee (the one nearest to the bracing blade). As with the low brace, practise the finishing blade position before fully committing to the high brace.

To help with the head position as you start to drive up with the down-edge knee, imagine you are drinking through a straw over the side of the kayak nearest the bracing blade.

13 USE OF SKEGS

Many sea kayaks have built-in skegs and, in my experience, the skeg is often underused by the paddler. The majority of kayaks when evenly laden will naturally turn head to wind. This is because the nose of the boat is anchored by the water it is cutting through while moving, allowing the unanchored tail of the kayak to be blown downwind. This effect is increased as the wind becomes stronger (unless the sea is so rough that the waves provide shelter from the wind).

The main use of the skeg is to provide extra resistance at the stern of the kayak from being blown downwind, making it easier to paddle in a straight line in windy conditions. Skegs are adjustable, allowing the kayaker to set the skeg to just the right depth in the water for the wind direction and strength. This requires fine-tuning and is not a simple skeg up or skeg down exercise. When using the skeg, make fine adjustments to its depth in the water until the least amount of correction is required when paddling forwards in the windy conditions.

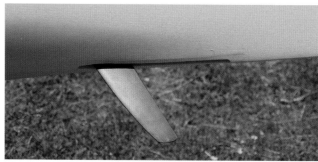

Retractable skeg in the down position and the slider control for skeg position.

SKEG UP

WIND

SKEG ¼ DOWN

SKEG ½ DOWN

SKEG ¾ DOWN

FULLY DOWN

Paddling into the wind the skeg is not required to maintain direction – skeg in up position.
Paddling with wind on front quarter – skeg in one-quarter down position to maintain direction.
Paddling across the wind – skeg in half down position. Paddling with wind on rear quarter –
skeg three-quarters down. Paddling downwind – skeg fully down to maintain direction.

Above is a general guide to how skegs can be set. Bear in mind that trim and kayak design will mean that your boat may not conform exactly to these principles. Use this as a guide and experiment. Different types of skeg can be lowered to different depths in the water. Use the images above as a guide to the amount of skeg to have down (e.g. a quarter, half, full and so on).

Using the skeg to turn

Once the concept of how the skeg works is understood, this knowledge can be used to help turn the kayak. When turning the kayak on the move in the wind, you will initially choose your turning stroke (see Chapter 8). To help this turning stroke, you can apply the skeg before, during or after the turning stroke, depending on the turn and wind direction.

- If you are turning the kayak upwind, then raise the skeg fully up to help the bow of the kayak turn upwind, allowing the stern to be blown downwind.

- If you are turning the kayak downwind, as soon as the bow of the kayak starts to move downwind fully lower the skeg. This will help anchor the stern and allow the bow to be blown downwind.

EQUIPMENT CONSIDERATIONS

The amount of skeg needed depends on the shape of the kayak hull, particularly for keeping it in a straight line in the wind. The way the kayak is packed will also have a big effect on how well the skeg works.

If the kayak has no skeg or the skeg breaks, then packing the kayak appropriately can help. The way we pack is an important consideration in any kayak, as the trim helps our kayak to perform as efficiently as possible (see Chapter 4).

14 USE OF RUDDERS

Overstern rudder in the up position. Overstern rudder in down position. A deck rope system to lower and raise the rudder.

Rudders are fitted as standard in some sea kayaks and are an optional extra in many. They have an up position when it has no effect on the kayak, for transportation, launching, landing or certain manoeuvres, and a down position for when being used paddling.

 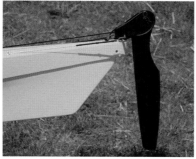 

The rudder can be adjusted when in the down position, usually by foot pedals, so that it can be set at different angles. Some foot pedals allow you to brace as normal with your feet and adjust the rudder by tilting it backwards. Other types will just move freely to adjust the rudder.

Rudder foot pedals that move freely can make manoeuvres which require pushing with the feet very difficult. Increased pressure on one foot will have to be counteracted with the other. This can limit performance and you may wish to consider buying a different type of foot pedal control.

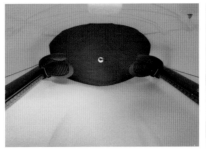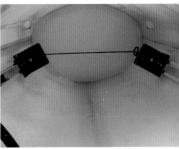

Altering the angle of the rudder will turn the sea kayak when it is moving forwards. If the rudder is set in a neutral position, it will act as a fully down skeg and anchor the stern, allowing the bow to move downwind. In windy conditions, when the kayak does not need to go downwind, the rudder angle may therefore need to be changed to turn the kayak upwind.

Advantages

The rudder has the advantage of turning the sea kayak or keeping it travelling straight in windy conditions, saving energy. It also allows paddlers with only a basic level of skill to manoeuvre the kayak in a variety of conditions.

Disadvantages

As the rudder is a mechanical device, it will need maintenance and can be damaged. If this happens, then the ability to paddle the kayak without the rudder is essential as well as the skill and equipment to mend the rudder.

The way the rudder turns the kayak puts a degree of drag on the stern of the kayak and this has a slight slowing effect. If the rudder needs to be set at an angle for a long time in windy conditions, energy could be lost compared to paddling with a well-set skeg or trimmed kayak.

The rudder also has a limited turning circle. There are many manoeuvres that are easier to perform by raising the rudder. Turning a kayak on the spot is the most obvious example of these.

A final key point is that a rudder needs some forward or backward speed on the kayak for the rudder to work. In windy conditions, when the paddler is not able to get the kayak moving at a reasonable speed, it may become impossible to turn. If this happens, the kayaker will need to be able to turn the kayak without the help of the rudder … or be at the mercy of the wind!

Forward turning using a rudder

The rudder keeping the kayak in a straight line. The rudder turning the kayak. Rudder angle for turn.

1 Set the kayak moving forward – forward paddle to get the kayak moving at a good speed.

● Ensure that the rudder is set in a 'neutral' position in order to keep the kayak in a straight line.

● Decide well in advance when you are going to turn; the rudder will turn the kayak gradually when applied.

● Plan a route that uses wider turns as opposed to tight turns whenever possible.

● With the kayak moving forwards, the rudder will work more effectively at a reasonable speed.

2 + **3** Apply the rudder – push the foot pedal (tilt or move it) to change the angle on the rudder.

● Apply the amount of pressure that gives you the turn you need.

● Push on right foot to turn right; push on left foot to turn left.

● No edge is required and the kayak will start to turn.

● Maintain constant forward paddling to keep the speed on the kayak.

Reverse turning using a rudder

The rudder keeping the kayak in a straight line. The rudder turning the kayak in reverse. Rudder angle for turn.

(1) Reverse paddle to get the kayak moving at a good speed.

● Ensure that the rudder is set in a 'neutral' position in order to keep the kayak in a straight line.

● Decide well in advance when you want to turn; the rudder will turn the kayak gradually when applied.

● Plan a route that uses wider turns as opposed to tight turns whenever possible.

● With the kayak moving backwards, the rudder will work more effectively at a reasonable speed.

● In reverse, the rudder will turn the kayak in a tighter turn as the rudder has immediate effect.

(2) + (3) In reverse, less foot pressure and therefore angle on the rudder will be required to turn the kayak in a similar shape of turn as when moving forwards.

● Apply the amount of pressure that gives you the turn you need.

● Push on right foot to turn the stern right; push on left foot to turn the stern left.

● No edge is required and the kayak will start to turn.

● Maintain constant reverse paddling to keep the speed on the kayak.

Tighter turns with a rudder

Effectively using sweep strokes on the move and edge with the rudder to make the turn tighter.

Once comfortable with using the rudder in forwards and reverse, it is possible to make the turns even more effective if required. This can be useful if needing to turn tightly among rocks or if needing a more efficient turn in windy conditions. The most effective and simplest way to do this is to add a sweep stroke on the move, as described in Chapter 8, while using the rudder to turn the kayak. This can also be done in reverse as described in Chapter 9. Consider using the extended paddle turn as described in Chapter 7. This will have great effect as many of the sea kayaks with rudders are designed with hulls to keep them travelling in a straight line. With experimentation, you may find that many of the turning skills described earlier in the book can help the performance of the rudder.

Reverse braced handbrake turn

The rudder will turn the kayak tighter in reverse than it does when going forward. We can apply the rudder in combination with a reverse braced handbrake turn, as described in Chapter 9, to produce a very efficient tight turn. This turn is best used if you need to turn around to paddle in the opposite direction or if the wind is preventing you getting enough forward speed to turn the kayak.

(Left) rudder angle for reverse turn.
(Right) reverse sweep edged turn and rudder being used together.

- Ensure kayak is moving backwards at a reasonable speed.

- Apply reverse sweep to initiate turn as described in Chapter 9.

- Depending on the speed and on your kayak, you may need to use more than one sweep for maximum effectiveness.

- If using a right sweep stroke, press on the left rudder pedal. If using a left sweep stroke, press on the right rudder pedal.

(Left) rudder angle for forward phase of turn.
(Right) reverse braced handbrake initiation.

- Apply reverse braced handbrake as described in Chapter 9.

- As forward braced handbrake is applied, change the rudder to the opposite angle to that used for travelling backwards.

- Keep appropriate pressure on both feet to maintain the rudder angle as well as the kayak on edge.

Reverse braced handbrake turn finish.

- Finish the turn as described in Chapter 9.

- Maintain a constant angle on the rudder to finish the turn.

- With the rudder further forward, sweep strokes may be required to maintain the speed and turn the kayak.

CONCLUSION

In this book I have described in words and pictures the many methods we have at our disposal to manoeuvre and paddle a sea kayak. Depending on the type of sea kayaking you do, you may not have a need for all the skills described. However, it is important to decide on those which are of use and become able to perform them well. If you are a committed sea kayaker who wants to be able to paddle in most conditions and environments, then you should find a use for all of the skills in this book. The key to success is to practise the skills; once you are comfortable in a calm setting take the skills out onto progressively more challenging locations. Unfortunately, although this book gives you a good head start, it is no substitute for getting out there, paddling and practising the skills. The only other shortcut I could recommend is getting some coaching from a qualified coach.

We have not looked at the additional skills required for the more advanced environments of tidal races, surf, tidal currents and windier conditions. The skills in this book are, however, the foundations for these skills. Being able to perform them well will make it easier to progress to such environments.

All that is left is for me to wish you well dancing in harmony on the world's oceans with your sea kayak. With practice, that old barge with a mind of its own should soon be a thing of the past.

Happy paddling!

INDEX

MORE SEA KAYAKING TITLES

Kayak Rolling, by Loel Collins – ISBN 0-9531956-8-6

Kayak Surfing, by Bill Mattos – ISBN 0-9547061-0-2

Scottish Sea Kayaking, by George Reid & Doug Cooper – ISBN 0-9547061-2-9

Sea Kayak, by Gordon Brown – ISBN 0-9547061-7-X

Sea Kayak Navigation, by Franco Ferrero – ISBN 978-1-906095-03-1

South West Sea Kayaking, by Mark Rainsley – ISBN 978-1-906095-05-5

The Northern Isles, by Tom Smith & Chris Jex – ISBN 978-1-906095-00-0

Welsh Sea Kayaking, by Jim Krawiecki & Andy Biggs – ISBN 0-9547061-8-8

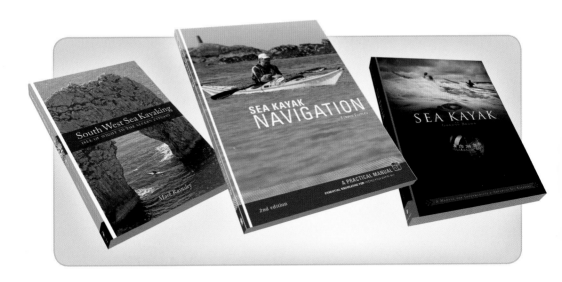

Pesda Press LTD
WWW.PESDAPRESS.COM

www.tideraceseakayaks.co.uk

TIDERACE
THE SPIRIT OF SEA KAYAKING

Scotland's NATIONAL
Outdoor Training Centre
inspiring adventure since 1948

glenmorelodge
a **sport**scotland national centre

Come sea kayaking with Glenmore Lodge

2 and 5 day courses for beginners to advanced.
Training and qualification courses for leaders / instructors.

Sea Kayaking trips around the globe

www.moln.fi

The World's Biggest Playground...

courses and equipment to
inspire your playtime

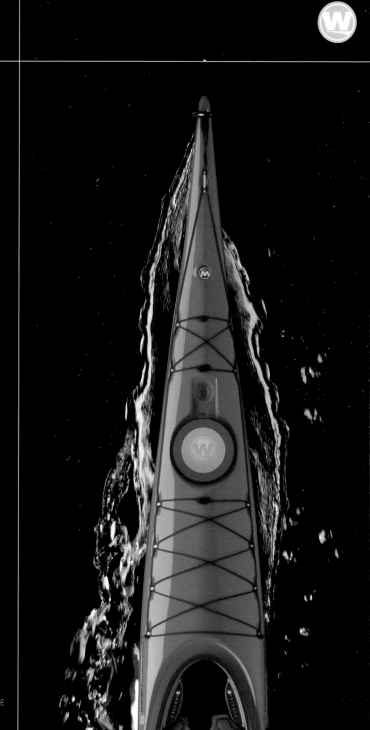

WILDERNESS SYSTEMS

CHASING PERFECTION

Unmatched tracking, maneuverability, control and comfort. Sleek, sophisticated exterior hiding engineering to handle the roughest conditions. With our new Phase 3® XP outfitting, ample storage, and height adjustable drop skeg, the Zephyr inspires those who demand the highest in performance.

See our 2009 product line and discover why our chase for perfection has made us the sport's most trusted name – in performance, quality, comfort, and owner satisfaction.

WhiteWater Consultancy International ltd.
The Old Village Hall, Bronwydd, Carmarthen, SA33 6BE
visit www.wwc.co.uk for more info

Freephone Hotline: 08000 15 15 20